Big PHAT
Goals

BE Progress

DEAN

How to Achieve

Big PHAT Goals

Goals

by Dean Lindsay

First Edition - 2018

ISBN-13: 978-0-9761141-4-7

Edited by: Jo-Ann Langseth
Cover Designed by: Jose Cordova

Quantity discounts are available on bulk purchases of this book for educational, gift purposes, or as premiums for increasing subscriptions or renewals. Special books or book excerpts can also be created to fit specific needs.
**For more information, contact:
Dean@DeanLindsay.com / 214-457-5656**

To Lena, my Love

Contents

"**People with goals succeed because they know where they're going.**"
— *Earl Nightingale*

Three more great quotes from American radio personality, speaker, & author, **Earl Nightingale** (1921-1989):

"The more intensely we feel about an idea or a goal, the more assuredly the idea, buried deep in our subconscious, will direct us along the path to its fulfillment."

"Whatever we plant in our subconscious mind and nourish with repetition and emotion will one day become a reality."

"Success is the progressive realization of a worthy goal or ideal."

Internalized Reasons Create Movement

Big PHAT Goals

The word **<u>MOTIVATION</u>** can be broken down into two root words:

Motive & Action.

<u>Motive:</u> an inner drive that prompts a person to act in a certain way. Motive is the goal or object of one's action. Other words for motive include reasons, purpose, intention.

<u>Action:</u> the doing of something. Examples of actions include: Do, rent, read, act, try, sign up, show up, eat, move.

<u>Motivation, therefore, is:</u> the inner drive to do, to try, motivation is the internal reasons to act.

Simply put: **Internalized Reasons Create Movement.** It is not a goal that motivates us, but our *internalized reasons* behind the goal that propel us to action.

"Strong reasons make strong actions."
— *William Shakespeare*

Often we fixate on a goal without giving enough focus and attention to the reasons behind the goal. Many of us do not need to come to terms with the world around us. Instead, we need to come to terms with our own unrealistic expectations and poorly defined goals.

Big PHAT Goals

Well-established reasons help us feel the internal pressure needed to focus. We must dig to the roots and remind ourselves of the benefits, the reasons behind the actions that will move us closer to our goals.

We need to do this for those we wish *to inspire to action* also. Being able to share with customers, prospects, coworkers, and employees how they will be able to move forward by partnering with us is a major key to personal and organizational goal achievement.

Each day we have the *choice* to move forward, to progress, to pursue our goals.

Big PHAT Goals

Crafting Big PHAT Goals hinges on strengthening our personal commitment to our goals by continually reminding ourselves of the personal benefits that reaching our and/or our company's goals will have in our lives.

The decision to be motivated to progress towards a goal is a personal choice.

I can't motivate you and you can't motivate me.
I may be motivational.
You may be motivational.

But truly, no one IS a motivator.
The only person who can motivate you towards accomplishing your goals is you.

"Motivation is a fire from within. If someone else tries to light that fire under you, chances are it will burn very briefly."
— *Stephen Covey*

The Progress Principle:

Everything we do is done because we believe, consciously, or more often subconsciously, that the projected consequences of those actions will be us feeling the unique, right mixture of six core feelings, feelings I call:

The Six Ps of Progress:

Peace of Mind
Pleasure
Profit
Prestige
Pain Avoidance
Power

Ever call up a buddy and ask,
"What are you doing?"
and they said, *"Nothing."*

You can't do "nothing." Doing nothing requires taking heavy medication.

Actually, taking heavy medication is still doing something. Sleeping is doing something. So is staring into space; so is flossing your teeth; so is scratching your arm; so is eating a plate of lima beans; so is waiting in the dentist's waiting room. We are always investing our time somewhere for some reason. We might not connect with the reasons consciously, but we are always doing something.

We have each said to ourselves at some point,
"Why am I doing this?"

Consciously or unconsciously, we choose to do
what we believe to be the best option at the
time. We may even know consciously that the
activity is not *good* for us but still we do it.
There are reasons.

They are our reasons. We may not
be able to vocalize them, or even
wrap our minds around them, but
we have reasons for the actions we
take.

The action may not be what we <u>wished</u> we would have <u>wanted</u> to take. Still, we chose to act (based on the circumstances and anticipated consequences). ***That is what personal regret is: wishing we'd have wanted to do something differently.*** When we look back upon actions we have regretted, we find that, at the time, we thought that taking the action would help us attain some mixture of the Six Ps of Progress… some unique mixture of:

pleasure, peace of mind, profit, prestige, pain avoidance, and power.

We regret the action because we did not receive the P's we expected, and/or because our actions deprived someone else of those good outcomes.

Have you ever heard someone say, "I don't have a choice"? Not true. We always have a choice, usually several. The choices may not be enjoyable, safe, or even legal, but there are always choices. Every choice has consequences. Maybe we view the consequences as unpalatably negative for us, but we do have choices.

The choices might not be choice choices, but there are always choices from which to choose *(that was a fun sentence to write).*

We don't have many **have to's**.
We don't *have to* kiss our spouse.
We don't *have to* work as a team.
We don't *have to* pray.
We don't *have to* smile, or even brush
our teeth.
We don't *have to* serve customers,
make sales calls or pay our mortgage.
We don't *have to* tie our shoes, feed our
pets, or hug our kids.
We don't *have to* pay for our kids' higher
education (*or for our pet's higher
education, for that matter*).

We don't *have to* eat.

You say,
"Wait a minute, Deano. We *have to* eat."

Are there people who chose not to eat? Yes.

What has happened to them? They died (painfully). It's still a choice. (If you know me, you know I choose to eat, kiss my spouse, hug my kids, pray, smile and brush my teeth for that matter.)

We do not *have to* pay our income tax. The consequences may include us going to jail but that is our choice.

We do not **have** to stop at stop lights. The consequences may include injuring ourselves and others – again, **our choice.**

We do not *have to* work. We've sold ourselves *(most would say rightfully)* on the idea that the benefits of working outweigh the benefits of not working. I asked a group I was working with once: *"Do you have to work?"*

Somebody yelled out,
"You do if you don't want to live in a tent."

I said,
"Are there people who choose to live in tents?"

They responded,
"Yeah. But I don't want to live in a tent."

I said, *"Exactly."*

These are choices that we are making.
There is power in that.

At each moment, we make decisions based on what we believe will help us feel the *Six Ps of Progress* – in the short term or long term.

<u>As an example,</u>

let's take an activity that most people would say they wish they didn't **have to** do –

mowing the lawn.

Why mow the lawn?

Maybe we want to have a good-looking yard like the neighbors do, and don't want to look like dirtbags. (*Prestige; Pain avoidance*)

Maybe it gives us a sense of accomplishment and a chance to think. (*Peace of Mind, Pleasure*)

Maybe we believe lawn mowing offers exercise. (*Pleasure, Pain Avoidance*)

Maybe we don't want to get fined by the city. (*Pain avoidance*)

Maybe a significant other "told" us to. (*Pain avoidance of not doing what significant other wants; Pleasure from pleasing significant other*)

Maybe we would rather keep our money than pay someone else to mow it. (*Profit, Pain Avoidance*)

How we judge the results is subjective. Having a well-groomed lawn offers progress for some. For others, amassing a noteworthy collection of vintage lipstick holders offers progress. There is always a result, an outcome.

We cannot

not

accomplish something.

Some shift in feeling attends everything that we do. There is a new normal. It may be only ever so slightly new, but it's new.

There is *some* profit in having a garage sale.

There is *some* power in punching someone.

There is *some* pleasure in eating a bag of *Pringles. (*I know it is not a *bag* of Pringles but what is it -- a cardboard sphere of Pringles? What? A *tube* of Pringles, I guess.)

We may not like or care for what is achieved, but there are outcomes and consequences – and these outcomes affect our next action.

Did the action (eating that sandwich, working for that company, using that wireless company, reading that book, wearing those shoes, buying that house) result in us feeling **<u>enough</u> pleasure, peace of mind, profit, prestige, and power?**

Did the action help us **avoid <u>enough</u> pain?**

There are outcomes for both parties when someone chooses to utilize our products and services. There are outcomes when someone decides not to utilize our products and services.

This is also extremely subjective. We value achievements, as well as gauge success, based on whether the time and effort invested in the activity help us feel *enough* of the Six Ps of Progress.

We can't choose nothing.

Choose Progress.

"Many people fail in life,
not for lack of ability or brains
or even courage but simply
because they have never organized
their energies around a goal."
— *Elbert Hubbard*

Big PHAT Goals

Three more great quotes from American philosopher, publisher, & artist, **Elbert Hubbard** (1856-1915):

"Know what you want to do,
hold the thought firmly, and do every day
what should be done, and every sunset will
see you that much nearer to your goal."

"To avoid criticism, do nothing, say nothing,
and be nothing."

"The greatest mistake you can make
in life is to be continually fearing you
will make one."

Let's Get Started... <u>Ponder & Progress:</u>
<u>The Reasons Create Movement Exercise</u>

1. Do you have strong reasons to take strong action? Why or why not?

_____

_____

_____

2. How are your reasons presently propelling you to action?

_____

_____

_____

_____

_____

3. How can you become more motivated and bound to your goals? How about team goals?

_____

_____

_____

_____

_____

4. How can you help others discover, realize, and embrace their own reasons for action?

_____

_____

_____

_____

_____

5. What is your WHY?

_____

_____

_____

_____

_____

_____

6. What are the reasons behind your movement?

_____

_____

_____

_____

_____

_____

7. What new strong reasons do you need to take strong actions?

_____

_____

_____

_____

_____

_____

8. How do you create inner drive?

_____

_____

_____

_____

_____

_____

9. How are you encouraging others to develop inner drive?

_____

_____

_____

_____

_____

_____

10. What are you motivated to do? Why?

_____

_____

_____

_____

_____

_____

"He who has a strong enough why can bear almost any how."

— *Frederick Nietzsche*

Defining Your Parameters for Progress

Big PHAT Goals

"**Whenever you want to achieve something, keep your eyes open, concentrate and make sure you know exactly what it is you want. No one can hit their target with their eyes closed.**"

— Paulo Coelho

Big PHAT Goals

Three more great quotes from Brazilian lyricist & novelist,
Paulo Coelho de Souza (1947-   ):

"There is only one thing that makes a dream
impossible to achieve: the fear of failure."

"You have to take risks.
We will only understand
the miracle of life fully when we allow
the unexpected to happen."

"When you want something,
all the universe conspires in
helping you to achieve it."

*What does **PROGRESS** mean to you?*

*What would bring you the most **pleasure, peace of mind, profit, prestige, power, and pain avoidance?***

What are your goals? Why?

What do you want out of life?

Big PHAT Goals

These important questions are far too often overlooked. I don't presume to know what you should want out of your day or your life, but I do know that our actions are futile if we don't know what *we really want.*

The following Parameters of Personal Progress exercise can be unnerving because we don't ordinarily take the time to think like this.

There is so much going on in our immediate day-to-day lives that we don't give ourselves a chance to reflect on our lives relative to the big picture.

Parameters for Personal Progress

a harsh 5 Minute, Five Step Exercise

Step One
Take a piece of paper and write today's date at the top but add **15 years**. Then write,

"Today I am _____."

and write your age but again add **15 years**. (Scary, I know.)

Step Two
Think of all you want to have accomplished within the **next 15 years.**

Step Three
Take a long breath in and
write nonstop for 5 solid minutes.

Write down everything you want to have done with your life in those 15 years.

Imagine that whatever you get down on the paper will happen, and what you do not get on the paper won't.

List experiences you want to have enjoyed, people you want to have helped, things you have acquired, qualities of character you have internalized. Include the things you want to stop happening, bad habits or bad feelings. You are the artist. Paint the picture. Dare to dream.

Big PHAT Goals

How do you envision your next 15 years?

What do you want to have accomplished?

What do you want to have seen or experienced?

Reach all sales goals or recruitment levels?

Want to get married? Stay married?

Have children? Put your kids through college?

*What cities and countries do you want
to have visited?*

Big PHAT Goals

Want to learn another language or two?

*Want to stop drinking, smoking,
eating fried foods?*

*Want to earn ten sales trips or win most
sales contest?*

*What musicians do you want to
have seen in concert?*

*Maybe you want to be in a play or
ride in a helicopter or start a non-profit?*

Any people you want to have helped? Who?

*Climb a mountain, run a marathon,
bench 200 pounds?*

Big PHAT Goals

Become a CEO, a Vice President or earn your master's degree?

Earn a black belt in Tang Soo Do?

Want to write a book or learn guitar?

Be awarded 'Best Team Member of the Year', three years in a row?

Want to donate to charities? Which charities?

Care for your parents in their old age?

Have a million dollars in the bank?

Maybe you want to visit the New 7 Wonders of the World?

Big PHAT Goals

Something Wonderful to know

The NEW 7 Wonders of the World, which were officially announced at a ceremony in Lisbon, Portugal, on July 7, 2007 (07.07.07), are:

Chichén Itzá, Mexico
Christ the Redeemer, Brazil
Machu Picchu, Peru
Great Wall of China
Petra, Jordan
The Roman Coliseum, Italy
The Taj Mahal, India

The Great Pyramid of Giza in Egypt is the only one of the original "Seven Wonders of the Ancient World" that still exists. It was decided that the Great Pyramid would not be included as one of the new Seven Wonders to offer it special recognition as the only remaining original World Wonder.

What do you want?

Life offers Choices.

Which are Progress and which are Change to YOU?

What are your Parameters of Personal Progress?

Did you do Step Three?
Did you really?

Step Four

Estimate how much time it would take to achieve each item on your list **if you started today.** *

A month?
Six months?
One year?
Five years?
Fifteen years?

* <u>*Hint:*</u> *Fifteen years is the max.*

a harsh Step Five

Go back to the top of the page and circle the year (plus 15) and your age (plus 15).

Those are the **only two facts** on the page.

Fifteen years from now: **that will be the year and you will be that age.**

The rest is up to you
(I told you it was a harsh exercise).

Big PHAT Goals

"When you know what you want
and you want it bad enough,
you'll find a way to get it."
— *Jim Rohn*

Two more great quotes from American entrepreneur and author, **Jim Rohn** (1930 - 2009):

"Discipline is the bridge between goals and accomplishment."

"If you don't design your own life plan, chances are you'll fall into someone else's plan. And guess what they have planned for you? Not much."

Big PHAT Goal-Crafting Defined

Big PHAT Goals

We must dedicate ourselves to ***<u>crafting</u>*** personal and organizational goals that are so attractive, so alluring to us, that we are ***compelled to progress*** by continually making choices that move us toward their accomplishment.

In short, *well-crafted goals are* **PHAT:**

P*RETTY*

H*OT*

A*ND*

T*EMPTING*

As a *noun*, **_craft_** can mean:
an object or machine designed for a journey, like a ship or an airplane.

As a *verb*, **_craft_** can mean:
to make or manufacture with skill and careful attention to detail.

A **_goal_** is:
the aim, the objective, the purpose, the point.

<u>Goal-crafting</u> is:

the practice of creating personal
and organizational targets that are
so clear, *so* well thought-out,
so enticing, *so* attractive,
so Pretty, Hot And Tempting
**that they actually become tools
or vessels in our journey to
their accomplishment.**

*Our lives and organizations will surely
change without well-crafted goals, but it
is doubtful that they will progress.*

Well-crafted, progress-based goals do not merely remind us of the desired destination; they help create the conditions and environment needed for their achievement.

Well-crafted, progress-based goals propel us into forward-focused action and strengthen our resolve to progress.

Six Rules of Big PHAT Goals Crafting

Big PHAT Goals

<u>Rule #1:</u>

Big PHAT Goals Are Written and Visualized.

Big PHAT Goals

"Believe you can and you're halfway there."

— *Theodore Roosevelt*

Theodore Roosevelt's
THE MAN IN THE ARENA

Excerpt from "Citizenship In A Republic" / France / 1910

"It is not the critic who counts; not the man who points out how the strong man stumbles, or where the doer of deeds could have done them better.

The credit belongs to the man who is actually in the arena, whose face is marred by dust and sweat and blood; who strives valiantly; who errs, who comes short again and again, because there is no effort without error and shortcoming; but who does actually strive to do the deeds; who knows great enthusiasms, the great devotions; who spends himself in a worthy cause; who at the best knows in the end the triumph of high achievement, and who at the worst, if he fails, at least fails while daring greatly, so that his place shall never be with those cold and timid souls who neither know victory nor defeat."

Written goals crystallize thinking, enhance commitment, and help identify the strong reasons that propel the strong actions. Having goals in writing gives them weight and more importance: for whatever reason, not only the conscious but the subconscious mind takes them much more seriously. Written goals are also vital when developing a course of action.

"If a man knows not what harbor he seeks, any wind is the right wind."
— Lucius Annaeus Seneca

The mind will not reach for achievement until it has clear objectives. Writing and frequently rereading goals turns on the "Can Do" switch in our brain, and the power to accomplish the goal begins to flow.

A study on goal-setting, conducted at Dominican University in California, found that we are 42 percent more likely to achieve our goals when we write them down. Goals that are written, read, rewritten, rephrased, and reread get impressed into our subconscious mind.

Often, what hinders our progress is not who we think we are, but who we think we can not become.

We may not know exactly **how** to go about achieving our goals, and our conscious mind may not even think them possible, _but if we write out our goals_ and visualize their accomplishment every day, our subconscious mind **will work** to make them a reality.

> **"The secret to accomplishing what matters most to you is committing your goals to writing."**
> — _Michael Hyatt_

Myth alert:

The "Yale Study of Goals" is often cited as a testament to the power of written goals. However, most scholars doubt the 1953 "study" ever took place. The so-called study claimed to have found that the 3% of Yale graduates who had written goals at the time of graduation were worth more financially twenty years later than the remaining 97% combined.

Too bad the "YSG" is probably an urban legend, because properly written goals are actually vital, and today it is estimated that fewer than 5% of us have properly written goals.

Let's get that percentage up by "getting down with" writing our goals down.

<u>Rule #2:</u>

Big PHAT Goals Connect to Personal Progress.

Big PHAT Goals

"What you get by achieving your goals is not as important as what you become by achieving your goals."
— *Zig Ziglar*

Two more great quotes from American author, salesman, and speaker, **Zig Ziglar** (1926 – 2012)

"A goal properly set is halfway reached."

"Your attitude, not your aptitude, will determine your altitude."

Often, individuals must make an organizational goal their own, as in a new technology rollout, reorganization, or a merger.

To get all team members (including ourselves) psyched, engaged and committed to the organization's goal, we need to dig into why & how the goal's achievement will benefit all involved *(via job security, bonuses, flex time, exciting new projects, raises, promotions, shorter commute, less stress, etc.).*

Highlighting the benefits creates true goal alignment.

Plainly put, each person involved in a goal's achievement must believe there is something favorable in it for him or her. We are unlikely to work toward a goal that we can not personalize as positive for us. If team members believe that the potential for progress is worth the effort, they will be more engaged and more readily take on challenges in support of the organization's goals.

For a goal to actually become a tool in its own achievement, it must generate genuine excitement when we envision its accomplishment.

How do achieving organizational goals mean Personal Progress for those who must act?

Whether the goal is meeting sales quota, buying a new boat, becoming more efficient in customer-service calls, or finishing a financial report, we must find ways to make the goal progress for us in some way.

When highlighting the reasons behind the goal, remember the Six Ps of Progress:
Peace of Mind, Pleasure, Profit, Prestige, Pain Avoidance and Power.

With that personal guidepost ever in sight, we stay committed to reaching the goal.

Why we want to achieve a goal is far more important than the goal itself.

Big PHAT Goals

<u>Rule #3:</u>

Big PHAT Goals Are Stated in Present Tense.

Big PHAT Goals

"If you want to be happy, set a goal that commands your thoughts, liberates your energy and inspires your hopes."

— *Andrew Carnegie*

Two more great quotes from Scottish American industrialist, **Andrew Carnegie** (1835 – 1919)

"People who are unable to motivate themselves must be content with mediocrity, no matter how impressive their other talents."

"The man who acquires the ability to take full possession of his own mind may take possession of anything else to which he is justly entitled."

Stating goals in the present tense tells our subconscious mind that we are committed – that the goals will not remain forever stuck in a future tense – as in, *I WILL be wealthy.* Our mind takes ownership, sees the goal as an actuality (rather than a potentiality) – *I AM wealthy* – and works toward its realization.

"Victorious warriors win first and then go to war, while defeated warriors go to war first and then seek to win."
— Sun Tzu

The subconscious mind chooses a path of least resistance. If we write, *"I will be debt-free,"* the subconscious mind does not act, because the "will" postpones the goal's achievement to some indefinite time in the future. When we craft goals as if they were already achieved, already true, our minds want to *make* them true.

Examples:

> *Daily, I am ...*
> *I surpass my sales goals.*
> *I know how to...*
> *My family and I are...*
> *I work well with others.*

Well-crafted goals, stated in the present tense, serve as powerful affirmations.

"Whether you think you can or whether you think you can't, you're right."
— *Henry Ford*

Think of affirmations as personalized powerful ads that you tell yourself over and over again about yourself and your life. Get over any weird thoughts you might have about affirmations – we all use them. If I were to ask participants in one of my sales, customer service, or team building programs, ***"Do you talk to yourself?"***

Some would say, ***"Yes"***

and some would think to themselves,
"Hmmm… Do I or don't I?"

We have lived our whole lives making affirmations. Unfortunately, affirmations are often self-critical and self-limiting:

I'm destined to be poor, stuck, unhappy.
I am not good at selling, prospecting, closing.
I am always tired, bored, getting sick.
I get frustrated with customers quickly.

Words are containers of Progress or Change, choose them wisely. Be careful about everything you say to yourself, or think to yourself, about yourself, because you'll end up being right.

Your brain is a terrible thing to use against yourself.

<u>Rule # 4:</u>

Big PHAT Goals Are Detailed and Measured.

Big PHAT Goals

"What gets measured gets improved."

— Peter Drucker

Three more great quotes from Austrian-born American management consultant, **Peter Drucker** (1909 – 2005)

"There is nothing quite so useless as doing with great efficiency something that should not be done at all."

"The best way to predict the future is to create it."

"Plans are only good intentions unless they immediately degenerate into hard work."

We are able to measure and track progress only toward goals that are detailed and specific. It is imperative that we craft goals with precise and vivid outcomes so that we can be sure we are progressing and not merely changing.

A vague, general, or conflicted goal produces vague actions and vague results. A specific goal produces specific actions and specific results. The more information we can give our subconscious mind about our intentions – *our wants, our goals* – the clearer the right next steps become, and the more focused our actions will be. It is fine if the goal takes many words to map out. The key is to crystallize our intentions.

For example, *"I have a new job"* is generic,
not very helpful, and certainly not very inspiring.
Most of us could get a *new job* within a week,
if not a day. It probably would not be a job
that matched our skills, paid well,
or that we even liked, but we could get *a job.*
So be darn sure to specify:

> *In what industry?*
> *What position and responsibilities?*
> *What pay range?*
> *What benefits, 401K, vacation?*
> *How much travel?*
> *How long commute?*
> *Company car?*
> *Work from home?*
> *What kind of boss (if any), and coworkers?*

The "specs" can go on and on.

Our general goals do little to propel us to specific action.

Yes, it takes time, but it is vital that we craft
our goals in as much detail as possible.
It is perfectly fine to rewrite the goal, refine it,
add to it, mess with it.

Becoming almost ridiculously particular about
what we want, and *why* we want it, helps create
the inspiration that propels us to progress
toward our goals – instead of focusing attention
on the countless other options of how we could
invest our time and energy.

Big PHAT Goals

<u>Rule # 5:</u>

Big PHAT Goals Are Positively Worded.

Big PHAT Goals

"Flaming enthusiasm,
backed up by horse sense
and persistence,
is the quality
that most frequently
makes for success."

— *Dale Carnegie*

Two more great quotes from American lecturer & developer of legendary courses, **Dale Carnegie** (1888 – 1955)

"Remember happiness
doesn't depend upon
who you are or what you have;
it depends solely on
what you think."

"Inaction breeds doubt and fear.
Action breeds confidence and courage.
If you want to conquer fear, do not sit
home and think about it.
Go out and get busy."

Words hold great power. They have since "the beginning." Crafted goals should focus our conscious and subconscious minds on future progress, not past problems and limitations. Therefore, we should craft goals that focus on what we want, not on what we don't.

Any words or phrases that have negative connotations perpetuate frustration, worry, and regret because they remind us of past weaknesses or failures.

In turn, this can create a mental block that limits our pattern of thought and behavior. It is helpful to become aware of when we're using defeatist words like ***can not, do not, will not, never.***

Big PHAT Goals

We need to rephrase our goal statements, eliminating any negative words and using believable, positive words.

Instead of writing, *"I don't eat junk food,"*

Write, *"I am a healthy eater. I eat foods that are good for me."* Then list healthy foods and why healthy choices are good for you.

Instead of writing,
"I will not stay up late, oversleep, and be late to work,"

Write, *"I go to bed by 10:30 p.m. each night and am on time for work each day."*

Then list five ways in which early to bed, early to rise, makes you *healthy, wealthy, and wise*.
There are three ways right there.
Thanks, Ben Franklin!

Crafting goals from a positive perspective raises our expectations and encourages empowering thought processes. We get our subconscious to work for us, opening up our options and making things seem possible and more doable.

The subconscious mind does not judge or argue; it only carries out instructions. The more positive the imagery we sow in our conscious and subconscious minds, the more positive results we will reap.

Big PHAT Goals

<u>Rule # 6:</u>

Big PHAT Goals Have an Achievement Date.

Big PHAT Goals

"No matter how carefully you plan your goals they will never be more than pipe dreams unless you pursue them with gusto."
— *W. Clement Stone*

Three more great quotes from American businessman, philanthropist & author, **W. Clement Stone** (1902 – 2002)

"Thinking will not overcome
fear but action will."

"When you discover your mission,
you will feel its demand.
It will fill you with enthusiasm and
a burning desire to get to work on it."

"Sales are contingent upon the attitude
of the salesman –
not the attitude of the prospect."

Achievement dates are vital for measuring and tracking our progress. Many of us waste a great deal of time talking about what we want to do, or to have, or to become, someday. *Someday is not a day of the week.**

Without an end date there is no strong reason to take strong action today. Having a specific time frame gives us the push, the prod, the sense of urgency to get moving.

Achievement Date
Or Procrastinate,
Set One and Get Moving
Before It's Too Late.
(I rhyme all the time.)

101

Without a date for accomplishment, we have only crafted a wishy-washy wish which floats around. We never get moving because we feel we can start at any time.

A realistic time frame helps reel the goal in and make it real. Grounding our goals within a realistic time frame gets the fire burning and sets our subconscious mind in motion.

"Goals are dreams with deadlines."
- Diana Scharf

Big PHAT Goals

Many of us have so many goals that we end up pursuing two dozen of them poorly, rather than three or four with laser-like focus and unflagging effort. Establishing achievement dates for our goals helps us decide which ones warrant the majority of today's time and energy.

Often it turns out that we have underestimated the true time, effort, and knowledge required to accomplish our goals. We run out of patience and passion, or lose sight of the goal's purpose. Most of our goals can be met if they have realistic achievement dates and we work to stay committed to them.

If we don't achieve our goal within our time frame, we can always set a new achievement date.

> **"The greatest danger for most of us is not that our aim is too high and we miss it, but that it is too low and we reach it."**
> — *Michelangelo*

* *Someday Is Not a Day of the Week* is the title of an insightful, motivating, and eye-opening children's book by Denise Brennan-Nelson. I recommend it highly.

Committing to Big PHAT Progress

Big PHAT Goals

"The quality of a person's life is in direct proportion to their commitment to excellence, regardless of their chosen field of endeavor."

— *Vince Lombardi*

Three more great quotes from legendary American football coach, **Vince Lombardi** (1913 – 1970)

"The difference between a successful person and others is not a lack of strength, not a lack of knowledge, but rather a lack of will."

"The harder you work, the harder it is to surrender."

"Individual commitment to a group effort – that is what makes a team work, a company work, a society work, a civilization work."

The hardest aspect of goal achievement is not in crafting a goal or even in knowing how to achieve it.

The real challenge is staying connected to the passion and understanding of WHY. Understanding the reasons behind our goal channels the passion in the right direction, or at least in *some* direction.

We initiate actions because, _in that moment_, we believe those actions will bring us the *Six Ps of Progress* with more intensity than any other option – short-term or long-term.

Whatever goal we craft, it needs to *LOOM LARGE* in our mind for us to continually work toward achieving it.

Will reaching your Big PHAT goal bring you more pleasure, peace of mind, profit, prestige, pain avoidance and power than any other actions you could take? **Why or why not?**

This concept is simple, but not easy. It is hard and even impossible to practice 24/7. It is very common to start our day committed to doing *this* and to not doing *that,* only to end up that day doing *that* and not doing *this*.

It's not that we forgot, or got confused. As the day wore on, what we were initially committed to shifted, and other things became more attractive, took precedence, seemed somehow more pressing to us.

We might stop taking steps toward a particular goal, but we are always moving toward outcomes that we believe will help us feel some unique mixture of:

Peace of Mind, Pleasure, Profit, Prestige, Pain Avoidance, and Power.

Though constantly reminded of *good* ways we could and should invest our time and money, it is easy to get led away from our goals.

Our heads can be turned by the immediate gratification we would receive by taking some other action, or even agreeing to pursue someone else's goals.

There are some benefits, be they ever so humble, to pretty much every activity.

Are there benefits in eating a jelly donut? Pleasure (by the ton) and short-term pain avoidance.

Big PHAT Goals

Are there benefits in not *eating a jelly donut?* Pleasure, pain avoidance, power, prestige, and profit.

Are there benefits in spending twelve hours a day at your job or running your business?

Are there benefits in taking a day or a week off?

Are there benefits in getting up early in the morning?

Are there benefits in sleeping in?

Are there benefits to you in handling everything yourself?

Are there benefits in delegating?

Are there benefits in working out?

Are there benefits in not working out?

Commitment is a moment-by-moment decision. Reminding ourselves about the pleasure, peace of mind, profit, and prestige we will enjoy, and the pain we will avoid by accomplishing our crafted goals, generates the commitment and motivation to do, reach, and act.

"With the power of conviction, there is no sacrifice."
— *Pat Benatar*

We live in a drive-thru society. <u>Beware the lure of Insta-Progress.</u> The opportunity for some level of instant gratification is all around us. If we feel the need for a little bit of pleasure, *boom!* There's a fast-food restaurant right around the corner. *Want to avoid some pain?* Just flip on the tube.

We are offered countless ways to take the easy road to some lesser form of progress. Without personal, healthy, short- and long-range personalized goals, we are at the mercy of any person or circumstance with a little weight, anything with some decent-sounding *whys.*

The Six Ps of Progress attached to our goals must be **PHAT**er & shine more brightly in our minds than the benefits of anything else we could do at that moment.

Don't remind yourself about a goal. *Remind yourself of the benefits of the goal.*

<u>Don't</u> tell or remind prospects about your product.

Share with them how your products help them progress.

<u>Don't</u> remind sales professionals of their sales goals.

Remind them about the money they will make, or the trips they will earn by reaching their sales goals.

<u>Don't</u> remind team members about the change needed.

Remind them of the progress achieved by making the change.

Sell yourself on the benefits of your goals.

Advertise your goals to yourself by posting the benefits - *how you will feel the Six Ps of Progress* - someplace where you will see them.

Effective advertising campaigns don't show us a product, they share how the product or service will positively affect our life – i.e., help us avoid pain, gain pleasure or feel prestige.

And ads don't just pop up ONE time. Advertisers *continually* remind us about the benefits of their products and services.

Ad agencies know the power of:

Repetition, Repetition, Repetition.

We must continually remind all involved how the goal *(company goal, sales goal, customer service goal, safety goal, or individual goal)* **is tied to personal progress.**

How can you advertise your Big PHAT goals to yourself?

Maybe you could "Carrey" around the reasons.
When actor Jim Carrey was just starting out in show business, he wrote himself a ten-million-dollar check for acting services rendered.
He carried this check in his wallet for years as he auditioned around Hollywood – to remind himself WHY.

We don't forget about our goals; we forget WHY they are our goals.

Our Well-Crafted Goals must be the Prettiest, Hottest, And Tastiest Goodies on the Smorgasbord of Life.

Ponder & Progress:
The Committing to Progress Exercise

1. Will your Big PHAT Goal's achievement bring you pleasure? More pleasure than anything else you could choose to do with your time? How? Why?

_____

_____

_____

2. Will your Big PHAT Goal's achievement bring you peace of mind? More peace than anything else you could choose to do? How? Why?

_____

_____

_____

3. Will your Big PHAT Goal's achievement bring you profit? More profit than anything else you could choose to do? How? Why?

_____

_____

_____

_____

_____

4. Will your Big PHAT Goal's achievement bring you prestige? More prestige than anything else you could choose to do? How? Why?

_____

_____

_____

_____

5. *Will your Big PHAT Goal's achievement help you avoid pain? How? What pain will you be likely to feel if you do not accomplish that goal? What is more painful –*
the <u>discipline now</u>, or the <u>regret later</u>?

_____

_____

_____

6. *Will your Big PHAT Goal's achievement bring you power? More power than anything else you could choose to do? How? Why?*

_____

_____

_____

7. What habits will you have to break to achieve your Big PHAT Goal? Why will you break them?

_____

_____

_____

_____

_____

8. What habits will you have to establish to progress towards your Big PHAT Goal?

_____

_____

_____

_____

_____

_____

Two Most Important Questions:

9. Are you truly, totally committed to your Big PHAT Goal? Why?

_____

_____

_____

_____

10. How are you continually reminding yourself of the reasons and benefits connected to your Big PHAT Goal's achievement?

_____

_____

_____

_____

Big PHAT Goals

Progress Takes Persistence

Big PHAT Goals

"Nothing in the world can take the place of persistence."
— *Calvin Coolidge*

Personal, professional, and social progress demands persistent action. The greatest goals, ideas, plans, and skills in the world are useless unless they are combined with a generous amount of persistence. Persistence is a byproduct of passion. Passion leads to a zest in the pursuit. To keep the passion, we must constantly remind ourselves of the benefits we are expecting from our efforts.

News flash: Goals <u>can</u> be achieved *without a plan.* It will most likely take us much longer, but we will eventually progress if we stay <u>*committed.*</u> The dangerous thing about not having a plan is that the longer it takes to progress toward a goal, the more likely we are to search out or give in to other ways to try to feel the *Six Ps of Progress.* Note that I said *other* ways, not better ways. And I said *try to feel*, not feel.

Without a plan, we are likely to get discouraged and give up. "Losing sight of the goal" means that it has not been defined clearly enough, and/or not held on to long enough, to be realized. A plan helps us achieve our crafted goals faster and more efficiently, without wasting resources or pulling our hair out.

It is not the plan that makes goal achievement possible, it is persistent action towards the goal and persistent action is initiated and sustained by strong, internalized reasons **(PHAT reasons!)**.

***Don't get me wrong,
I am a firm believer in planning,
but our best-laid plans will not get
us <u>where we are not committed</u>
to going.***

Keeping our thoughts constantly on the reasons behind our goals is the stimulus that keeps us committed and able to dispense with setbacks quickly, and to decisively redirect our efforts.

"Nana korobi ya oki"

is a popular Japanese saying that vividly expresses the importance of persistence, despite setbacks.

As the proverb teaches, the eventual winners are those who **"fall down seven times, get up eight."**

Every moment that we focus on the strong reasons that have inspired our goals, the closer we are to taking determined action toward their achievement.

134

"Making miracles is hard work. Most people give up before they happen."

— Sheryl Crow

The key is to not let reasons for pursuing other goals steal our attention, become PHATter, or more compelling.

We must keep our focus *(and our employees', customers', and prospects' focus)* on the Six Ps of Progress that will be felt in accomplishing the goal.

The Progress Challenge Riddle *(a classic)*

If there are five frogs on a log and three decide to jump off, how many frogs are still on the log?

Answer: **Five.** *Deciding is not <u>doing</u>.*

Decided to make sales calls?

We may have decided to make a sales call, and it may even play out very nicely in our minds, but until we pick up the phone and dial, we are not making sales calls.

And we can't let a misguided desire for perfection stop us. **We don't have to be perfect to *Be Progress*.** We can always improve our technique, improve our plan and our actions.

Progress does not demand perfection, only persistence.

Things can and do go wrong.
Missed opportunities should not be allowed to become big emotional "downers."
Never make self-pity part of your makeup.
We must reframe setbacks to our advantage.

Most "successful" people say they learned more from their failures than their successes because they were eager to learn what went wrong and to avoid repeating it.

Being persistent does not mean being bullheaded. **If what we're trying isn't working, we must take a fresh approach.**   Consider that by eliminating another idea that didn't work, the path to progress became clearer.

When things go wrong, we can let Thomas Edison light our way. Asked if he was discouraged after thousands of attempts at creating a viable light bulb had failed, he replied: *"Why would I feel like a failure? And why would I ever give up? I now know definitively over 9,000 ways that an electric light bulb will not work."*

138

On a regular basis, be sure and invest time in revising your plan. Creating a feedback loop is vital – even if we're the only ones in the loop.

Fill days with action toward crafted goals. Start and, if we get sidetracked, we must acknowledge that the reasons for pursuing some other goal or goals have become stronger in our mind.

Then is the time to ask: *Why?*

Big PHAT Goals

If the promise of our goals no longer propels us to action, we need to do a gut check.

Are they still our goals?

_____

_____

_____

_____

Are the reasons strong enough, PHAT enough, to propel us to persistent action?

_____

_____

_____

_____

Each step toward a goal is progress. It is powerful for us to appreciate all that we're doing to stay on track, and to express our gratitude to those who are helping and supporting us.

Find ways to enjoy the journey.
Pat yourself on the back. Reward yourself.
These are <u>our lives</u> we are talking about here.

"What man actually needs is not a tensionless state but rather the striving and struggling for some goal worthy of him. What he needs is not the discharge of tension at any cost, but the call of a potential meaning waiting to be fulfilled by him."
— Dr. Viktor Frankl

Four more great quotes from Austrian neurologist,
psychiatrist, and Holocaust survivor,
Dr. Viktor Frankl (1913 – 1970)

"Everything can be taken from a man
but one thing: the last of the human freedoms—
to choose one's attitude in any given set
of circumstances, to choose one's own way."

"Between stimulus and response there is a space.
In that space is our power to choose our response.
In our response lies our growth and our freedom."

"Each man is questioned by life; and he can only
answer to life by answering for his own life; to life
he can only respond by being responsible."

"Live as if you were living a second time,
and as though you had acted
wrongly the first time."

<u>Ponder & Progress: Progress Takes Persistence</u>

1. How are you reminding yourself of the benefits of your Big PHAT Goals?

_____

_____

_____

_____

2. What steps have you taken today toward your Big PHAT Goal?

_____

_____

_____

_____

143

3. *What actions could you take today that would be progress toward your Big PHAT Goals?*

_____

_____

_____

_____

4. *What activities will you trim back or cut out to achieve your Big Phat Goals?*

_____

_____

_____

_____

_____

_____

5. What do you need to do, learn, or become to progress?

_____

_____

_____

_____

_____

_____

6. How will you begin acquiring the new skills you need to progress?

_____

_____

_____

_____

7. Which new people do you need to build relationships with?

_____

_____

_____

_____

_____

8. What is working? What have you learned?

_____

_____

_____

_____

_____

_____

9. *What new obstacles are there?*

_____

_____

_____

_____

_____

_____

10. *How will you become more persistent?*

_____

_____

_____

_____

_____

_____

"Without deviation from the norm, progress is not possible."

— *Frank Zappa*

Teaming Up for Big PHAT Progress

(Goal Alignment & True Employee Engagement)

"Give me a stock clerk with a goal and I'll give you a man who will make history. Give me a man with no goals and I'll give you a stock clerk."
— *J.C. Penney*

Big PHAT Goals

Four more great quotes from American businessman and entrepreneur, **James Cash (JC) Penney** (1875 – 1971)

"Growth is never by mere chance;
it is the result of forces working together."

"As a rule, we find what we look for;
we achieve what we get ready for."

"In every man's life there lies latent energy.
There is, however, a spark that, if kindled,
will set the whole being afire, and
he will become a human dynamo,
capable of accomplishing almost anything
to which he aspires."

"The well-satisfied customer will bring
the repeat sale that counts."

Each of us has personal goals.
The organizations we team up with - *work for* -
have organizational goals. This is not a
problem. This is actually great news.

One of the most effective ways to progress
toward our personal goals is by teaming up
with organizations to achieve organizational
goals.

We work / team up with a company or
organization because we believe that by
accomplishing team goals, we take steps closer
to our personal goals. If we didn't believe that
way, we wouldn't - or at least shouldn't - work
there *and probably won't work there for long*.

True, the relationship between employee and employer is sometimes one of conflict, with a worker doing a particular job because they need the money and don't think they can get anything better elsewhere.   But at every level, everyone works to personally progress. Even the CEO is there because she believes that by partnering with the company, she takes solid steps toward her own personal goals.

Organizations are only as strong as their team members' personal goals and the team members' belief that the organization's progress helps them progress toward those goals.

People without personal goals are "no show" employees, poor salespeople, and inconsistent customer-service professionals. That's a major reason that teenagers sometimes don't make the best employees. It's not because they are lazy (though some are, as are some adults) or do not have any work ethic.

It's because they generally don't have strong reasons connected to the work they do. On the other hand, let's say that a 15-year-old boy wants a car on his 16th birthday and he has to buy it himself. He is committed to getting that car.

Will he be a reliable employee? **Likely, yes.**

Why? Because he is committed and connected to the outcome of the work. He is teaming up to reach *his* goal by reaching *the organization's* goals!

For teams to progress, team members must believe that they are personally progressing. Team members must believe that as they strive to accomplish team goals, they are taking steps toward their own personal goals.

If a company's goals don't line up with its team members' personal goals (and vice versa), neither is likely to be reached.

True goal alignment strengthens employee engagement!!

Sales managers should love it when
their sales professionals:
> *buy a new house,*
> *have their eye on a boat,*
> *or decide to have another kid,*
> because now that person has some strong
> reasons to take strong action.
> They have strong whys to get out there
> and **sell.**

When our company has a new product rollout, is
merging with another company, or has a new
way to get business moving, it is natural to think,
Oh, no! Here comes something else I have to
learn. Something else I have to do.

But think about it. Wouldn't it be far worse if the leadership within our companies said,
"We have no new ideas on how to be profitable.
We have no new ideas on how to progress.
Go get 'em, tiger!"?

We should be glad, excited, and even relieved about new initiatives, because the decision makers (who should know a thing or three) believe they have ideas that will help the company progress, and in turn help us to progress.

Without our "work," we would still have our personal goals. Even if we were "trust-fund kids," we would have to find some other way to take progressive steps.

We team up with our organizations because we have goals, and through our partnering we take steps to achieving them. Companies with solid, well-thought-out organizational goals make it easier for us to achieve our goals. The company helps us progress as we help the company progress.

Team Up for Big PHAT Progress!

Ponder & Progress:
Teaming Up for Big PHAT Progress

1. Why do you "work?"

_____

_____

_____

_____

2. How are you helping your organization reach team goals?

_____

_____

_____

_____

_____

_____

3. How is your organization helping you reach your Big PHAT Goals?

_____

_____

_____

_____

_____

_____

4. How are you progress for those you "work" with? How do you offer the Six Ps of Progress?

_____

_____

_____

_____

5. *What are two of your organization's goals?*

_____

_____

_____

_____

6. *How can working toward these organizational goals become steps toward your Big PHAT Goals?*

_____

_____

_____

_____

_____

_____

7. How will accomplishing these organizational goals accelerate the achievement of your Big PHAT Goals?

_____

_____

_____

_____

_____

_____

8. How does your organization help you avoid pain?

_____

_____

_____

_____

9. What organizational initiatives have you resisted that could lead to your personal progress?

_____

_____

_____

_____

10. How does teaming up to accomplish your organization's mission statement help you feel the Six Ps of Progress?

_____

_____

_____

_____

_____

"If everyone is moving forward together, then success takes care of itself."

— Henry Ford

The Little Mind That Could

One evening, several years ago,
as I was listening to our elder daughter,
Sofia, read Wally Piper's classic
The Little Engine That Could to her younger
sister, Ella, it occurred to me what a powerful
little story it is. In his book, Mr. Piper shares
the story of a little red engine pulling a train
"filled full of good things for boys and girls"
on the other side of a mountain.

When the little red engine breaks down,
a toy clown hops off the little train and starts
asking larger passing trains if they will help.
The first two trains refuse to help because
they feel they are too big and important to
pull toys and goodies.

A rusty third train relates that he is too old and tired to help, and chugs away saying, **"I can not. I can not. I can not."**

Finally, a little blue engine passes by and stops immediately when she sees the clown waving. The little engine's first words are,

"What is the matter, my friends?"

The clown relays the challenge, and the little blue engine explains that she has never been over the mountain. She then sees the tears in the dolls' eyes and thinks of the good little girls and boys who will not have any toys to play with or good food to eat unless she helps.

She looks at the mountain and says, *"I think I can. I think I can. I think I can."*

The little blue engine hitches herself to the little train and starts tugging and pulling and pulling and tugging. Slowly, the train moves forward.

"Puff, puff, chug, chug, went the Little Blue Engine. **'I think I can. I think I can. I think I can. I think I can. I think I can. I think I can. I think I can. I think I can. I think I can.'"**
— *from* The Little Engine That Could
by Wally Piper

Up they go, ***ever so slowly***
to the top of the mountain.

When they reach the top,
the toys cheer.

After coming down the mountain and unhitching
the train, the little blue engine chugs away,
saying happily,
***"I thought I could.
I thought I could.
I thought I could."***

The conviction that we have the power to progress is a major key to progressing. Remember, ***our brains want to be right.***
**Whatever the mind believes,
it will work to make true.**

But, the little blue engine didn't say, *"I think I can,"* only one time.
She said it over and over and over and over.
Repetition, repetition, repetition.

What do you think that little blue engine will say next time she is asked to pull a train over a mountain? Will she say, "I think I can"?

I think not.   She will say, ***"Yes, I can."***

Also, the little blue engine did not say, *"I think I can,"* and then glide away. She said it and immediately hitched herself to the little train and started **tugging and pulling and pulling and tugging.**

To progress towards our Big PHAT Goals, there must be

ACTION.

No dallying! The little blue engine had to **tug and pull** to reach her goal.

Will some of the progressive action steps that you will need to take to climb that mountain and reach your Big PHAT Goals be painful?

Yes.

Again, consider:

What is more painful to you, discipline or regret?

Finally, the little blue engine had strong reasons to climb the mountain.

She saw the tears in the dolls' eyes and considered the little children, who would not have any toys or good food to eat unless she helped.

She would feel pain if she didn't help, and would gain pleasure, prestige, and power if she did.

Develop strong reasons for taking strong action.

Remind yourself often of the personal benefits that reaching your and your company's goals will have for your life.

Help others develop strong reasons, so they too choose to take strong actions.

Progress is a step forward.
Take today's step.

Be Progress.

About Dean Lindsay:

With over seventeen years of experience helping build Engaged, PROGRESS-Based Sales Leadership and Customer Service Cultures, _Dean Lindsay_ has been hailed as a **_'Outstanding Thought Leader on Building Priceless Business Relationships'_** by _Sales and Marketing Executives International_ as well as a **_'Sales-and-Networking Guru'_** by the _Dallas Business Journal._

His books, **CRACKING THE NETWORKING CODE** & **THE PROGRESS CHALLENGE** have sold over 100,000 copies worldwide and been translated into _Chinese, Hindi, Polish, Korean, Spanish and Greek._ Dean has had the privilege of sharing his sales leadership and customer service insights in numerous countries including: _Sweden, Poland, Spain, Turkey, Ecuador, Venezuela, and the islands of Aruba and Jamaica._

Dean's clients include: _New York Life, Ericsson, Gold's Gym, Aramark Canada, International Customer Management Institute, UCLA Anderson School of Management & Haggar Clothing._

Continued...

Big PHAT Goals

A Cum Laude graduate of the *University of North Texas*, Dean served on the advisory board for UNT's Department of Marketing and Logistics.

Dean is also an award-winning songwriter, a marathon runner, a founding member of the ***Texas Shakespeare Festival***, and an alumni of ***Up With People***, the legendary international organization that bridges cultural barriers and creates global understanding through service and a rocking musical show - *Dean's cast was the first to perform in the Soviet Union.*

Bits of Trivia about Dean: He was *LeAnn Rimes* on-set acting coach on both a Hallmark Movie of the Week and on the soap opera ***Days of Our Lives*** and he played the role of one of the 'bad guys' in the Warner Brothers' blockbuster **TWISTER** *(Dean urges you to not look to hard for him in the film however, sharing that 'the flying cow ended up with a big part than I did.").*

His wife Lena, and their two strong and wonderfully nutty daughters, Sofia & Ella, live in the Dallas/Fort Worth Metroplex.

Contact Dean at: Dean@DeanLindsay.com & 214-457-5656

*Praise for **Dean Lindsay**'s book*

Cracking the Networking CODE:

4 Steps to Priceless Business Relationships

"This is ___a book that everyone will wish they read 20 years ago___. What a tremendous asset it would be if we could only memorize all of the quality pointers in this book."

> — *Frank Bracken, former President & COO*
> *Haggar Clothing Co.*

"Perhaps the most powerful way to leverage and multiply your talent and ability is by expanding your personal and business network. ___This book shows you how___."

> — *Brian Tracy*
> *Legendary Sales Trainer & Author*

"___Dean Lindsay is a master of progress___, and in this book will show you how to be the same. He'll take you by the hand – a pleasurable experience, because the man is an awesome writer – and ___lead you into the land of networking nirvana___."

> — *Jay Conrad Levinson,*
> *Father of the **Guerrilla Marketing** Movement*

Praise for the Work of
Dean Lindsay

"Dean Lindsay is *truly one of the best and most insightful speakers out there*. I have hired him, heard him and read his work. He is *always top notch with profitable tips and strategies* – plus he is fun to watch. Dean Lindsay rocks!"
— *Paul Rosowski, Regional Sales Vice President, Teknion*

"We hired Dean Lindsay to speak to our group about great customer service, but he did more… *he SHOWED us exceptional service*. Dean spent countless hours understanding our business, our customers and our service mantra. He quickly became a part of our team and was able to communicate our vision to employees around the world. *Our company hired a keynote speaker but got a life-long business partner and resource for our team*!"
— *David Webster, CEO, Electrical Components International*

"We recently had the opportunity to have Dean come speak at a Global Service Meeting. We appreciated the fact that Dean took the time customize his presentation to focus his vast experience on our goals. The *feedback from the attendees was OUTSTANDING*! Dean was humorous, energetic, and very relatable – everyone walked out re-energized too!! We would highly recommend Dean for any event and plan to have him back soon."

— *Greg Pressly, Vice President of Customer Operations, MetroPCS*

"*Dean Lindsay was the perfect choice* to keynote the Meineke Dealers Association Convention. His combination of *contagious wit and sales and service insights inspired us* to face the challenge of improving our operations, while providing us the template to make it happen."

— *Chris Schmitz, President, Meineke Dealers Association*

"Dean *brings a great sense of how to connect quickly* with people through impactful and fun stories, *I highly recommend Dean*."

— *Jim Snow, President, Gold's Gym International*

"Progress is a step forward. Take today's step."

— *Dean Lindsay*

Be Progress.

Dean Lindsay's Topics, Workshops & Coaching Programs Designed to Help Build Engaged, PROGRESS-Based Sales Leadership and Customer Service Cultures include:

- **How to Achieve Big PHAT Goals:**
  Teaming Up for Big PHAT Progress
  Fostering True Employee Engagement & Goal Alignment
- **Be a BAM!:**
  Keys to Becoming a Business Attraction Magnet
- **Cracking the Networking CODE:**
  4 Steps to Priceless Business Relationships
- **The PROGRESS Challenge:**
  Working & Winning in a World of Change
- **Celebrating Service Excellence:**
  *Featuring the **Cherishing Customers / CARE Model** & **ForWORDs & BackWORDS**:*
  Words & Phrases That MOVE Business Communication
- **Diving For Referral Pearls:**
  Cultivating Quality Referrals
- **Welcoming the Rise of Progress Leadership:**
  Change Management is Dead!